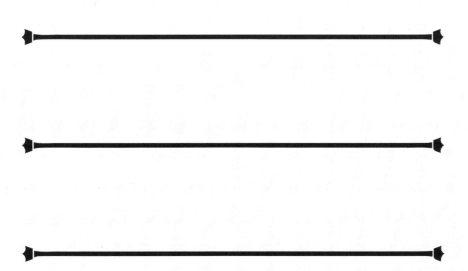

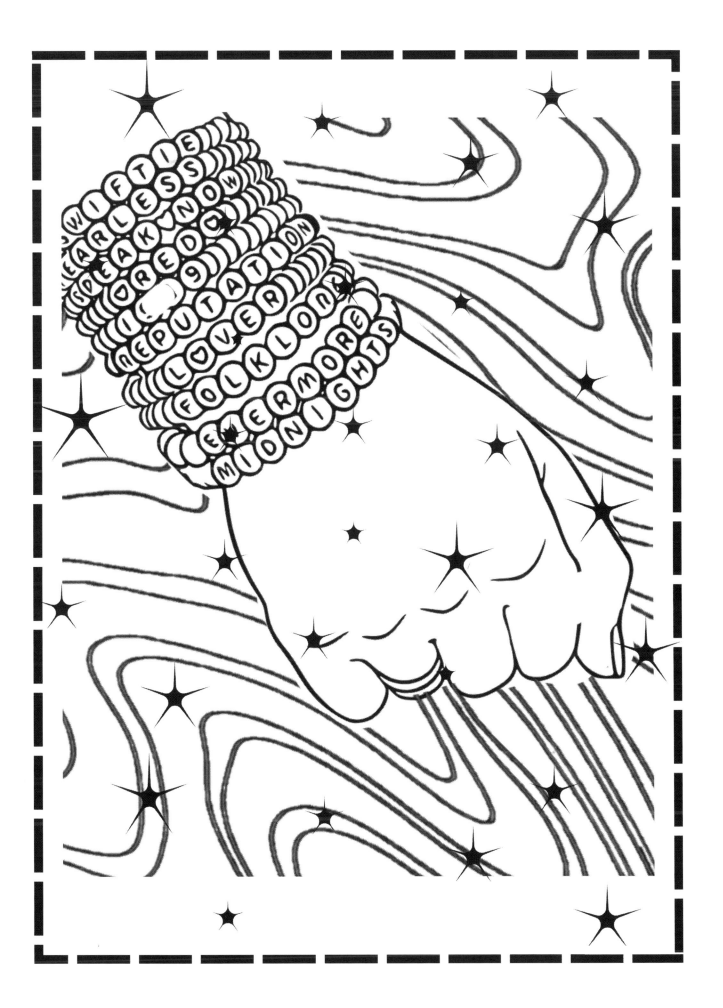

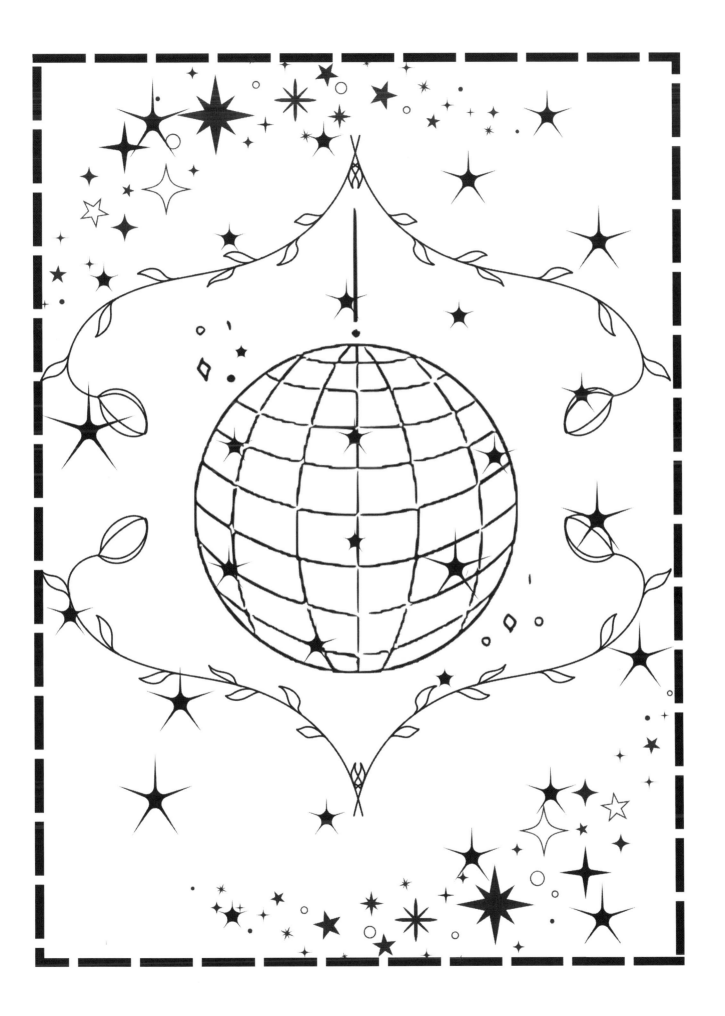

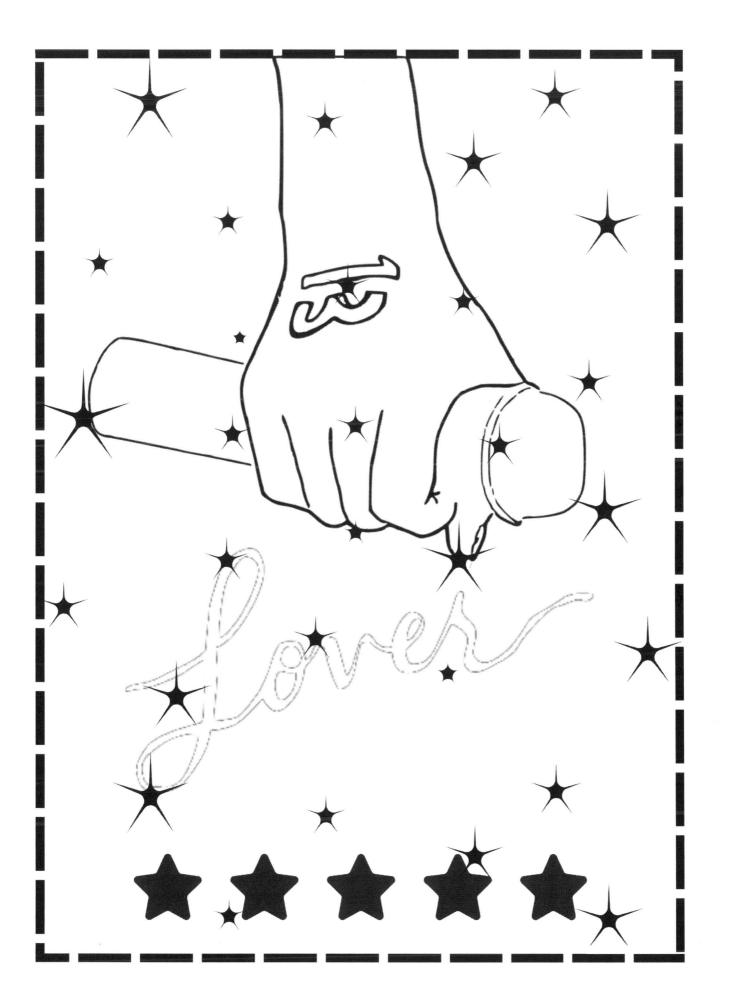

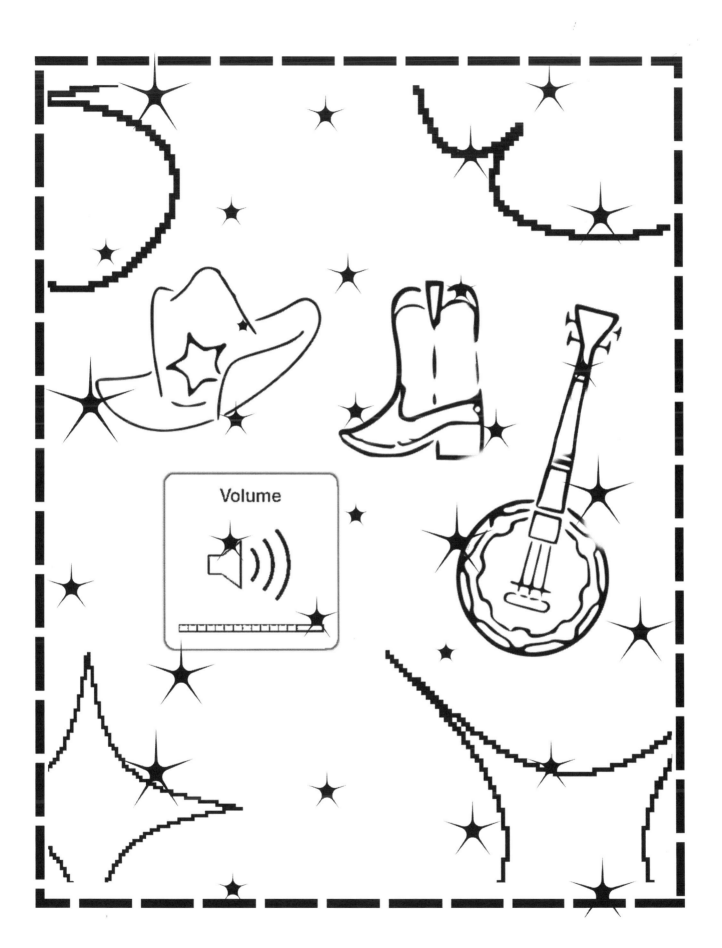

Volume

Band-aids don't fix bullet holes.

You put me on and said I was your favorite.

You call me up again just to break me like a promise.

"We don't need to share the same opinions as others, but we need to be respectful."

"Life isn't how to survive the storm, it's about how to dance in the rain."

"You only get so many firsts, each one is a blessing."

13

"Unique and different is the new generation of beautiful. You don't have to be like everyone else."

"People are going to judge you anyway, so you might as well do what you want."

FACTS

Her favorite dessert is cheesecake.

FACTS

Taylor wrote a 350-page novel when she was 12, which, so far, has never been published.

FACTS

Known for a love of cats.

FACTS

Taylor is extremely talented; she can play the guitar, piano, ukulele, electric guitar, and banjo!

FACTS

Birthday is on December 13th.

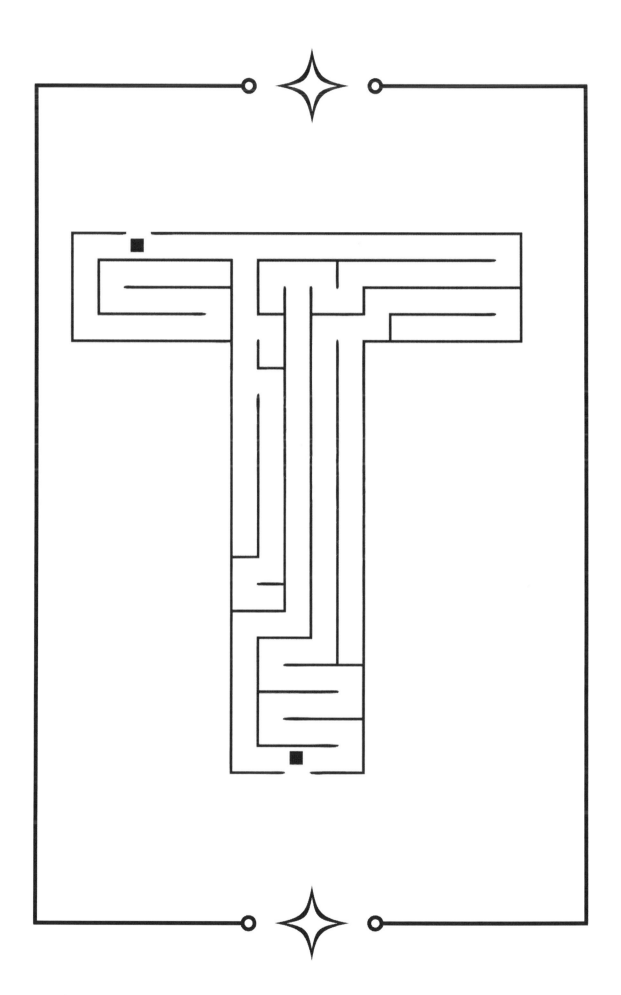

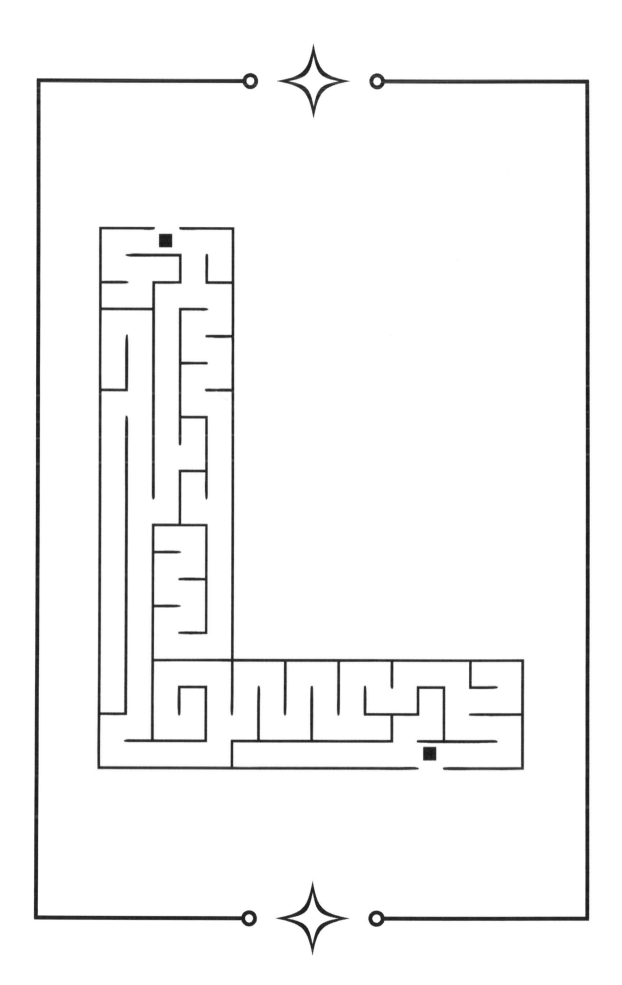

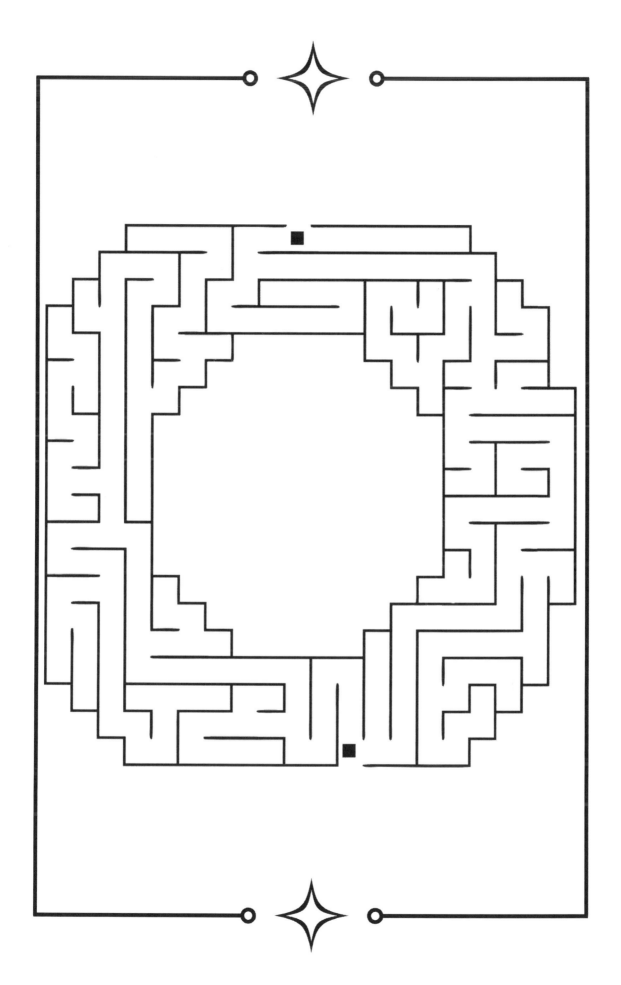

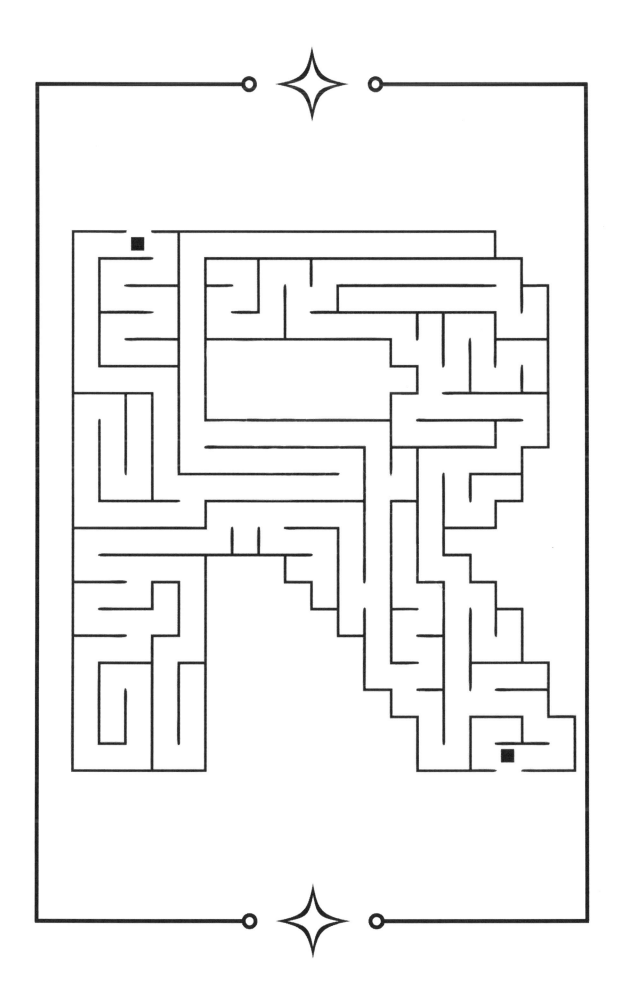

Solutions

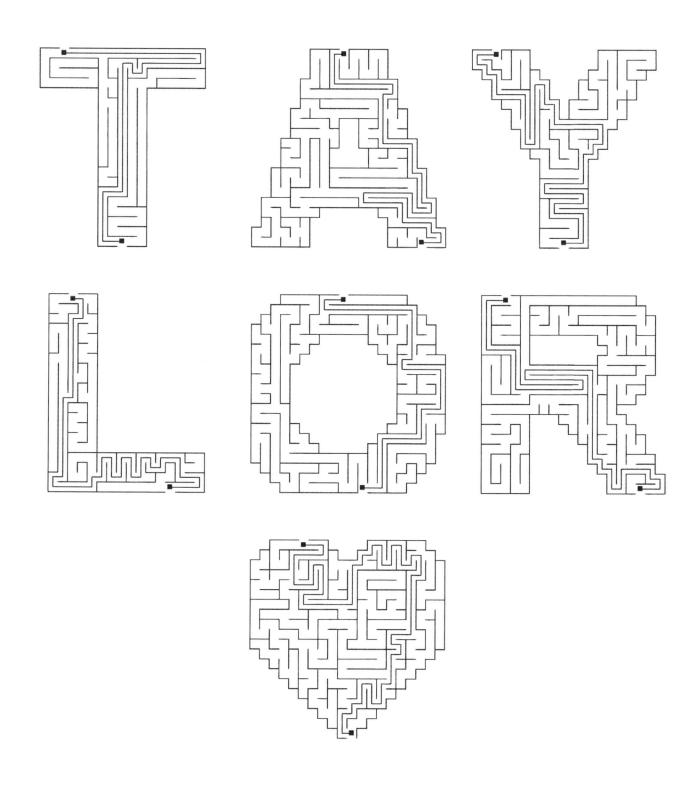

Made in United States
Troutdale, OR
11/25/2024

25272179R00053